HAL•LEONARD
INSTRUMENTAL
PLAY-ALONG

AUDIO ACCESS
INCLUDED

TENOR SAX

Disney Movie Hits

2	Belle
4	A Whole New World
6	Prince Ali
8	God Help the Outcasts
9	Hakuna Matata
10	Beauty and the Beast
12	Cruella De Vil
14	When She Loved Me
15	Kiss the Girl
16	If I Didn't Have You
18	Go the Distance
19	Circle of Life

To access audio visit:
www.halleonard.com/mylibrary

4644-2484-2345-6461

ISBN 978-1-634-04383-3

Disney characters and artwork © Disney Enterprises, Inc.

WALT DISNEY MUSIC COMPANY
WONDERLAND MUSIC COMPANY, INC.

DISTRIBUTED BY

HAL•LEONARD®
CORPORATION

7777 W. BLUEMOUND RD. P.O. BOX 13819 MILWAUKEE, WI 53213

Visit Hal Leonard Online at
www.halleonard.com

BELLE

From Walt Disney's BEAUTY AND THE BEAST

Lyrics by HOWARD ASHMAN
Music by ALAN MENKEN

TENOR SAX

3

A WHOLE NEW WORLD

From Walt Disney's ALADDIN

Music by ALAN MANKEN
Lyrics by TIM RICE

TENOR SAX

5

Slowing

Tempo I

PRINCE ALI

From Walt Disney's ALADDIN

Lyrics by HOWARD ASHMAN
Music by ALAN MENKEN

TENOR SAX

7

GOD HELP THE OUTCASTS

From Walt Disney's THE HUNCHBACK OF NOTRE DAME

Music by ALAN MENKEN
Lyrics by STEPHEN SCHWARTZ

TENOR SAX

HAKUNA MATATA

From Walt Disney Pictures' THE LION KING

Music by ELTON JOHN
Lyrics by TIM RICE

TENOR SAX

BEAUTY AND THE BEAST

From Walt Disney's BEAUTY AND THE BEAST

Lyrics by HOWARD ASHMAN
Music by ALAN MENKEN

TENOR SAX

CRUELLA DE VIL

From Walt Disney's ONE HUNDRED AND ONE DALMATIANS

Words and Music by
MEL LEVEN

TENOR SAX

WHEN SHE LOVED ME

From Walt Disney Pictures' TOY STORY 2 – A Pixar Film

Music and Lyrics by
RANDY NEWMAN

TENOR SAX

KISS THE GIRL

From Walt Disney's THE LITTLE MERMAID

Lyrics by HOWARD ASHMAN
Music by ALAN MENKEN

TENOR SAX

IF I DIDN'T HAVE YOU

Walt Disney Pictures Presents
A Pixar Animation Studios Film MONSTERS, INC.

Music and Lyrics by
RANDY NEWMAN

TENOR SAX

GO THE DISTANCE

From Walt Disney Pictures' HERCULES

Music by ALAN MENKEN
Lyrics by DAVID ZIPPEL

TENOR SAX

CIRCLE OF LIFE

From Walt Disney Pictures' THE LION KING

Music by ELTON JOHN
Lyrics by TIM RICE

TENOR SAX